the flap pamphlet series

Humaning

open, read, turn

Humaning

the flap pamphlet series (No. 27)
Printed and Bound in the United Kingdom

Published by the flap series, 2021
the pamphlet series of flipped eye publishing
All Rights Reserved

Cover Design by Petraski
Series Design © flipped eye publishing, 2010

Author Photo © Sylvia Suli
First Edition
Copyright © Laurie Ogden 2021

What We Are Given won the 2021 Ambit Poetry Prize, judged by Kim Addonizio. It will be published in Ambit Pop: 245.

The Land Was Burnt and *Hunger* were published in the BYP anthology *'An Orchestra of Feathers and Bone'* in 2017.

Someone's Father, Someone's Brother, Someone's Son was published in bath magg Issue 4, 2020, and *The Birds* was published in bath magg Issue 7, 2021.

The Birds was also published in Orion anthology 'Everything is going to be alright', edited by Cecilia Knapp, 2021

A previous version of *Maeve Tells Me She Programmed It to Never Rain in The Sims* was published in Dear Damsels in 2020.

Love Sonnet in the Aquarium was published in Anthropocene 2020

ISBN-13: 978-1-905233-73-1

Supported using public funding by

ARTS COUNCIL ENGLAND

LOTTERY FUNDED

Humaning

Laurie Ogden

'A human being is only breath and shadow' -

Sophocles

*'And although I don't understand my dreams, I know somewhere
There is hope, there is hope, somewhere there is hope'* -

Benjamin Clementine

Contents | *Humaning*

One

Two

Three

One

What We Are Given

I opened the matryoshka doll
and out came a grandmother, faded, coughing. I opened the grandmother
and out came a mother as a sobbing child, locked in a cupboard.
    I opened the mother
and out came a money spider which, hopeful, I opened
and out came an envelope that paper-cut my finger as I opened the letter
and out came a north-westerly wind that tore through the house, ripped off the roof,

to find me cowering in the bathroom, considering opening
me, I opened my mouth
and out came a banshee wail made of echoes, circling, a cycle, a cyclone.

I forced the doll shut but I'm still spitting echoes into the sink.
Let it end, let it end. Let it end
with me.

There Is a Hyacinth in Her Room
After Caroline Bird's 'Mystery Tears'

When she got the seeds no water or plant food
could coax them out of the soil. She didn't sleep.
She trawled internet forums to find
something, anything.

You suppose that's where she got the idea.

When she saw the first delicate spiral reaching
out from the soil she committed to the ritual;
inserting a small glass tube just under the collarbone,
distilling the joy out from her and into the soil.

There are hammocks under her eyes now.
The weight alters her vision; she holds
fleeting comments by their throats,
squeezes insults out of them.

You don't know how to hold her.
You ask if she would enter the plant
into a local gardening competition.
She stares at you blankly.

You can only assume the plant has grown in size.

The Land Was Burnt

The locals spoke Spanish at my sister's olive brown skin,
laughed when they realised she was not one of them.

The land was burnt so the flights were cheap.
Forest fires had run through the island,

finally released. A red bikini and almost-breasts.
Wear a t-shirt left in a crumpled pile at the water's edge.

Later, I lathered cream on my whimpering
chest, blushing and cracked on first exposure.

The Older Sister Is Moved to Point Guard

For Caitlin

a thirteen-year-old giraffe baby beats back
every shot you take on the basketball court
her new limbs   a few years from graceful
are a clumsy plié   you can't teach her
how to use them   or flat-pack her
back to child   take her home safe
you take another shot   her hand
an eclipse   shrinks you   close to redundant
oldest used to be synonymous with tallest
she's been watered so well

When the Police Officer Asks the Little Girl What She Saw on the Way Home From Dance Class

two men in the middle of the street
crumpled on top of each other
misshapen toes
in a pointe shoe

a couru across the chest
pointe-pointe-pointe-pointe
on a t-shirt
ripped like raffia
too too strange
a performance
a man assembled on the floor

when the car door opened
offbeat, improvised
one was lying still
the other's hand glinting
bottom of a tap shoe
and a 1-and-2-and-3-and-4
metal suzy-q-ing
in and out of his chest

there was no music

and we were watching
wishing we could
stop-time

The Weather Is Wearing Her

All the lads in the parks have taken their tops off and I'm jealous. They are a chorus line of nipples saying *y'alright?* to the sky. Apparently, I've got bombs for rose petals. I've packed them away as instructed but the man on the bus stares anyway. Maybe they are too dangerous to take on public transport. I decide to walk to you instead. This means I end up swelting into the pavement like a shit interpretive dance of an ice lolly in Malta. From the puddle of me, I watch her (me) stroll, half-decent sketch of a confident person, into the gallery/park/pub. From across the table you count, out loud, the freckles on my right shoulder.

Ode to Maud Wagner

Maud Wagner (1877-1961) was an American circus
performer and the first recorded female tattoo artist in the US.

I covet your confidence,
woman with your own name
inked on your left arm.
You poked a thousand ways
to own your skin,
and everything held within it.
Gut, brain, lung,

womb, heart, lust.
You pushed your daughter
through the eye of a needle,
until your body
was your own again.

You won't allow her father
to ink her. You forbid
her from carrying a man's
name, before she learns
to live in her own.

Two

Hunger

I want to tell her that her lipstick is red.
I want to tell her that her lipstick is red
and that her lipstick is looking at me.
I want to tell her that I believe her lips are that red
underneath the lipstick the lipstick
and when she breathes out
it almost sits on my collarbone.

She talks about a house she used to share
with her girlfriend.
I want to tell her that her lipstick is red
and that I am glad she had at one point
at least
a girlfriend.
She talks about the creative process
and I imagine her covered in paint
and nothing else
just animal, animal red
and I don't want to touch her
just to watch her dance in acrylic
painting her heartbeat onto the outside of her body.

Her friend asks her a question and she puts wine to her lips.
I think of red, and red,
and she puts the wineglass down too fast
and I want to ask her how she holds
her girlfriend but she is talking
about a husband,
who she holds, I imagine,
and children,
and I hear what she meant by girlfriend,
and I fight the urge to demand
that she gives me her lipstick

so I can eat it
all-in-one-go
say that was why I was looking
cheeks red now
red red
say
that was all I was hungry for

Uncomfortable

After Terrance Hayes' 'Nuclear'

They asked you to force a truce
with your body. They said you would urn
yourself, or that you would be unable
to conceive, your belly an uninhabitable nebula.
Your collarbone is a beacon
but there is a *how did you lose it* clamour
from the girls at the lunch table.
Your bones are a mob, their forte
disappearing you and calling it *unfat*.
You don't mention heaving yourself nuclear
on the toilet floor.

An Aviary

Nobody would know, not when you have your clothes on.
You take off your skin the way others would peel off
a rain-soaked jumper. Burrowed beneath your ribcage
a hawk stares with sharp eyes the same brown
as yours. It beats its wings, cautiously rhythmic.
The doctors mistake it for a heartbeat.

It was born like you were, an egg inside a woman's body
or maybe you swallowed the egg whole
the way other children eat watermelon pips.

You did show someone once. He mistook your ribcage
for prison bars, the hawk for your prey not predator
and, repulsed, backed away from you.

He is now with a woman who always stands naked,
confuses skin for pink lace, wears her bones on the outside
like the hoops of a dress. Finches and bluebirds
and pretty things flit to her, mistake her nipples
for petals, her sweat for raspberry drops.
She looks like she is being kissed forever.

The Rules of Elimination

Latrice Royale, RuPaul's
Drag Race: lip syncs Aretha,
hammocks a pretend bump, *you make
me feel like a natural woman.*

Someone must have
told her she could
throw her head back,
wail. Some days break

me. Feel like a natural woman
is a difficult mantra when
you shove pillows under your
shirt, loving what is gone.

The Mushroom Woman

The mushroom woman gouged a muscle out of her own thigh, placed it on the countertop in front of the nurse. The nurse took a few moments before looking up from Candy Crush. When she saw the upturned cap, red raw gills exposed and oozing, she screamed, ran from the room shouting for the doctor. The mushroom woman sat down to wait, as she had done for years.

When they took the mushroom woman away to bandage her up, a porter was called to wipe down the nurse's desk. When he got there, the surface and adjacent wall were flush with fungi. No matter how hard they scraped at it, it would not leave.

Someone's Father, Someone's Brother, Someone's Son

Last night we watched the latest episode of *Giri/Haji*, waiting for the backstory of why the lead woman was afraid of her ex partner. I say, *I hope he doesn't hit her,* by which I am also saying , *I hope you never hit me,* by which I am not saying that you have shown any inclination towards violence but the men on the screen of various backgrounds and cultures are eager to see what is on the inside like rabid children unwrapping the gifts of each other's skins and we all know it is only a little fiction and it is hard to say, *not mine, he's not like that,* whilst wondering how much my voice sounds like women in the recordings of themselves in the years months weeks days hours minutes before bruises form and are seen and renewed and even after.

Dog-Walking for Women

After R.A. Villanueva & Anne Byrne

Because we trail the canal path I cannot alone.
Because I walk with a greyhound in a muzzle.
(Because he slurps chicken bones but it makes him look badass.)

Because man with the pond-scum-smirk sees the greyhound.
Because threat black eyes stare man down.
Because I have told the greyhound everything. The man guesses this
Because man's away-footsteps are an irregular heartbeat.

Because he imagines the dog, ex-racer, set loose,
Because he replays this wolf pinning him down in the dark.
Because teeth on throat.   Because teeth on throat.

Because hand on throat.
Because down this path the only one who could save him is me.
Because I won't.

Your First Laugh

didn't know that good girls
laugh in corners
that good girls laugh
into cupped hands
that clever girls hold their laughter in
like buoys.

Three

The One Where I Bargain to Bring You Back

"What is grief, if not love persevering?" — Vision (WandaVision, 2021)

In an alternate universe where nobody has died
that I know, people are still grieving,

               so I move again,

this time to a universe where the people I know,
nobody they know has died,

            repeating this process

until eventually I'm sitting in Greenwich Park,
next to a Roman guard who insists the government

should bring back coliseums. I whisper to my reflection
in his stupid helmet that this is not what I meant

to do,

      I just dreamed of bringing you back

again, for the first time
   in years.

Maeve Tells Me She's Programmed It to Never Rain in the Sims

Where we   are

the successful
lesbian power couple.   Us two,
white picket fence.

                                                          Back in this
                                 sunny   universe we are
                                                          on the sofa
                                                          in our jammies.

Sim Maeve is a professional
chef, I've written seven hit
novels. She has overfed me   but

                                 here   Maeve knows
                                                          the cheat code

so bought Sim me
a swimming pool
to reset my shape.

                                                          Maeve has always
                                                          been someone
                                                          who should run
                                                          the show.

                                                          Back in this universe,
                                 we ask   *is this it?*
                                                          of the dirty dishes,
                                                          spend our Sunday cleaning.

Sim me has made herself sick   with stress.

         We are   watching anything with
                    Sarah Lancashire in it.

Sim Maeve makes her a cake.

          We talk about moving
          back to the North.

Sim me has started   glitching,
Swimming   fully
clothed.

The Birds

My friend bleeds on the picnic blanket.
She reaches down, expecting the damp
of a spilt tinny but feels warm, sees red.

We flock to cover her stained summer
dress, magicians releasing doves
from our pockets; tissues, make-up
wipes, sanitary pad. We waddle,
a gaggle, to the park bogs.

From the sky perhaps we are one
bird, the drunkest a beak squawking,
two of us for wings, two for tail feathers
and her, the bleeding beating heart.

Object Permanence

You have started reaching for me
when you are asleep. Stroke shoulder,
cup butt cheek, grab a twist of hair
or, sometimes, poke in the eye.

You used to dream I was running.
That used to make me uncomfortable.
This is softer, less *you're leaving,*
more child reaching for a blanket.

I used to pretend that you need
this more than I do. Every night
you convince me that I am real.

Love Sonnet in the Aquarium

That shark is a motherfucking big one.
That shark could quickly eat your mother whole.
A mother says *How ugly* to her son.
He ignores her, reaches out five-year-old
fingers pressed against the glass, the same star-
fish spread that mine have. We are both in love
now, in this moment with a shape that far
exceeds its 'that' name. It isn't enough,
just like Joe, the builder, is more than Joe
or a builder. How shadows of surfers
and seals are confused. This feeling will go
soon enough. We cannot take love further

like this. The shark taps on the glass signing
I heard that lots of humans are dying

Notes

There Is a Hyacinth in Her Room was written in a workshop led by Gabriel Jones, in response to Caroline Bird's poem *Mystery Tears* from her collection The Hat-Stand Union.

Uncomfortable is a 'Gram of &s', a form devised by inimitable Terrance Hayes. The 'Gram of &s' form consists of 11 lines. The final word of each line is an anagram of the title.

The Rules of Elimination is a tidal swell, a form I devised in the Barbican Young Poets workshops led by Jacob Sam-La Rose & Rachel Long. It consists of three stanzas, syllables 6789, 444, 9876. The fourth line of the first stanza and the first line of the third stanza (9 syllables) mirror one another. Anna Kahn was the first person to publish a poem in this form; her beautiful poem *Curtained Off* can be found on Dear Damsels.

Dog-Walking for Women was inspired by the form of Anne Byrne's poem *'Petition to Hackney Council to Re-Open London Fields Lido'* in the Barbican Young Poets anthology *'For Those with Collages for Tongues'*. Her poem was written after R.A. Villanueva.

Love Sonnet in the Aquarium is a Shakespearean sonnet. I promise it rhymes, or at least it does if you have a northern accent.

Acknowledgments

There are too many people to name who have supported me over the years. I hope you all know who you are, & how much you mean to me. I want to say thank you to some people who are particularly responsible for this pamphlet coming into existence:

To you, for reading. To Jacob Sam-La Rose, for years of imparting wisdom & encouragement as mentor, editor & friend. To all of the Barbican Young Poets community, especially: Bayan Goudarzpour, Victoria Adukwei Bulley & Joshua Judson, for your notes & fierce encouragement.

To the Brax fam: Gabriel Jones, the first person to truly believe in my writing, who helped me begin to believe, Maeve Tierney, Crispy Brown & Keit Bonnici, you beautiful humans who helped make me a better person. To Gabriel Akamo & Jeremiah Brown, my OF best pals & OG editors. To Mrs Perrin, for opening more doors than you realised. To Michael Bolger & the Poetry Takeaway, for being the main reason I could stay in London & for changing my life - I owe you a million pints. To all of 'Spare the Poets' Roundhouse Collective. To all of my writing peers who have become friends. To all of my family. And especially, to Fred & Duck, for everything, always.

Without you all this pamphlet wouldn't exist, and without you I wouldn't be me.